THE CHICK-O-SAURUS

KELLY CRULL

National Geographic
Washington, D.C.

DO YOU SEE THAT?

Dinosaurs hatched from eggs like birds.
WATCH OUT, THOUGH!
Baby dinosaurs grew fast.

LOOK!

Could this egg belong to a

VELOCIRAPTOR?

Velociraptors may have laid blue-green speckled eggs just like blackbirds and magpies.

We're in big trouble if it's an

ARGENTINOSAURUS.

They were as tall as a six-story building, longer than a basketball court, and as heavy as a space shuttle.

THERE IS A DINOSAUR
I really, really hope it's not a
TYRANNOSAURUS REX,
the giant meat-eating dinosaur with a bite that could crush a car!

LOOSE

IN THIS

BOOK!

HE HAS A VERY LONG TAIL,

That sounds like a

DIPLODOCUS!

Their tails could be as long as a school bus and snapped like a whip to stun their opponents.

RAZOR-
SHARP
CLAWS,

It's got to be a
UTAHRAPTOR.

They used their claws as hooks to snare their prey, pin them down, and eat them alive!

BONE-CRUSHING

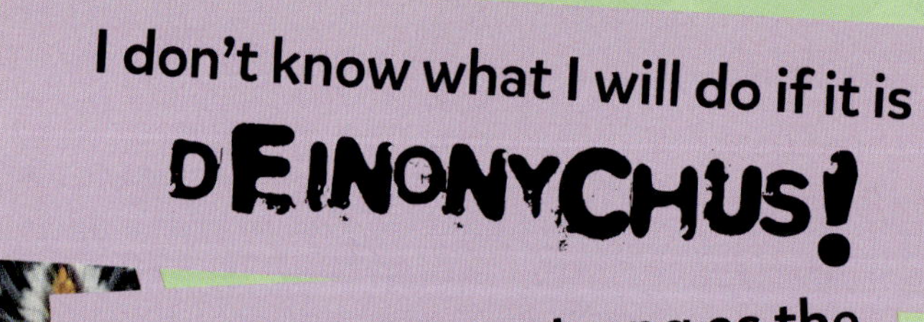

I don't know what I will do if it is a

DEINONYCHUS!

Their bite was as strong as the weight of 40 bricks pressing down on you.

JAWS,

AND SPIKES ON TOP OF HIS HEAD.

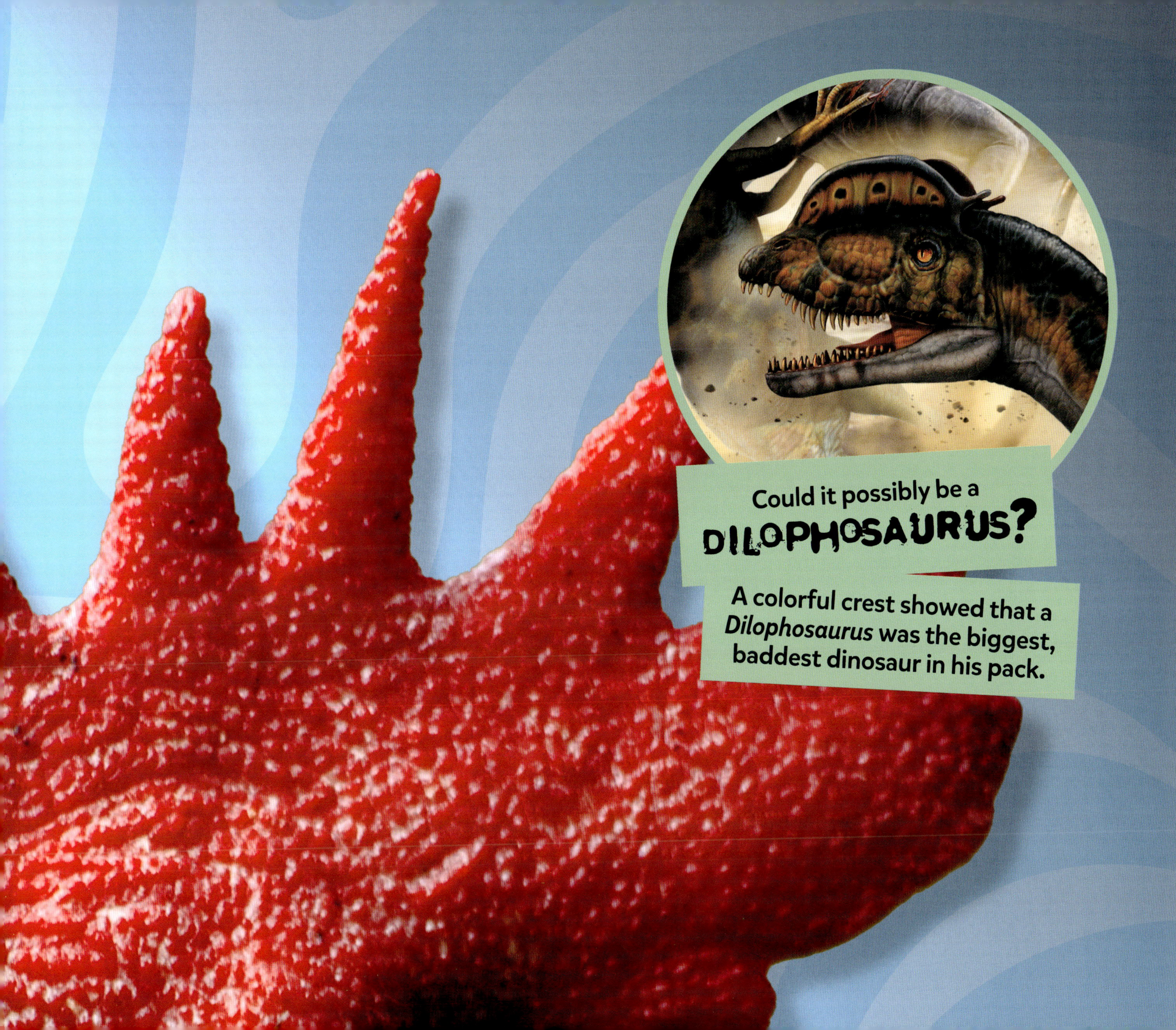
Could it possibly be a
DILOPHOSAURUS?
A colorful crest showed that a *Dilophosaurus* was the biggest, baddest dinosaur in his pack.

HE BEATS HIS MIGHTY WINGS AND SCANS THE HORIZON FOR FOOD.

MAYBE IF

WE ARE

VERY STILL

AND VERY

QUIET,

HE WON'T NOTICE US.

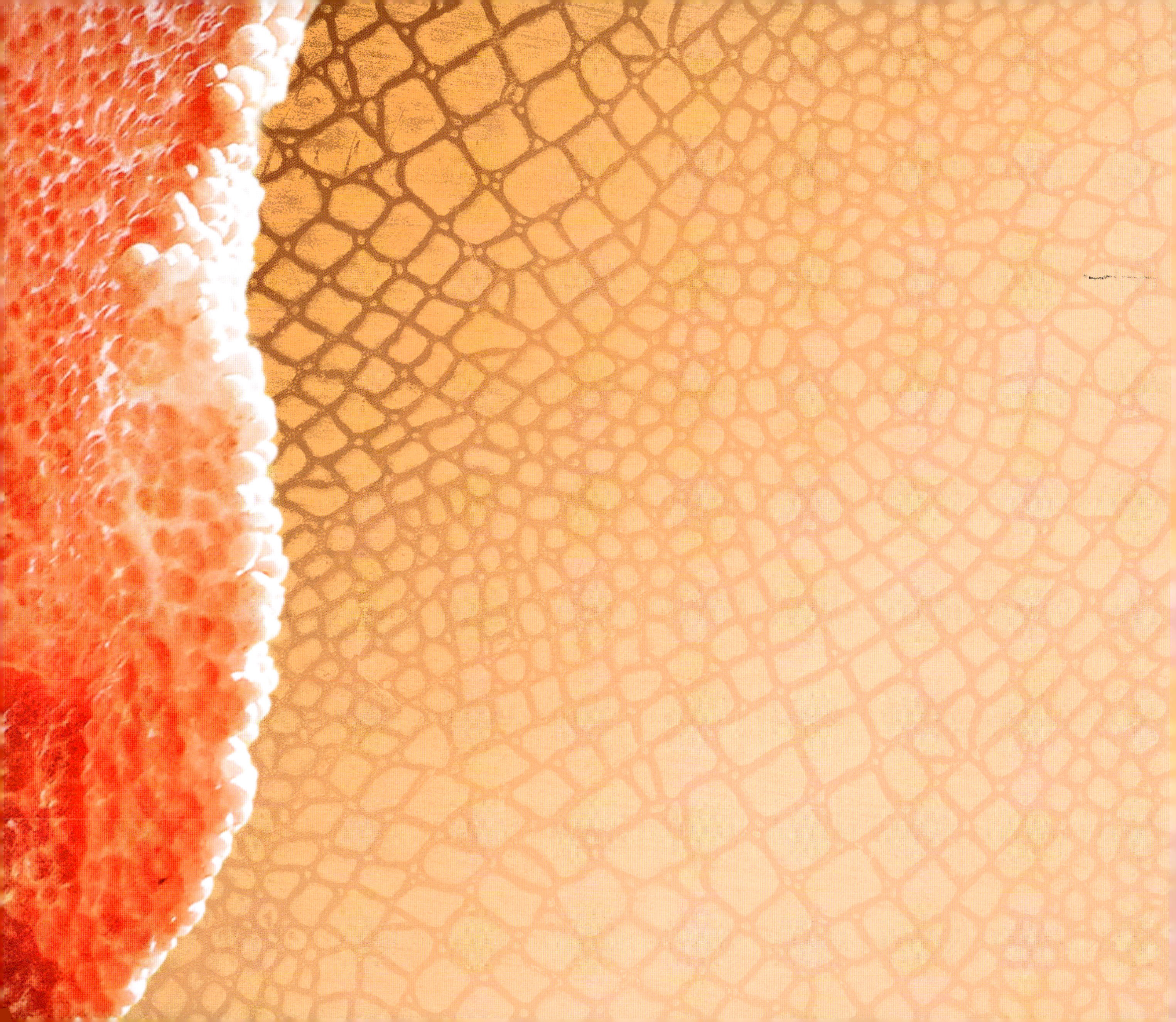

WATCH OUT!

HE'S GOING TO ...

COCK-A-
DOODLE-
DOO!

THE MIGHTY CHICK-O-SAURUS DEVOURS HIS PREY.

Did you know CHICKENS ARE DINOSAURS, TOO?

The fossil of a prehistoric bird called ***Archaeopteryx*** was discovered in 1861. A few scientists noticed the fossil of the bird looked like the fossil of a dinosaur called ***Compsognathus***. Both had two legs, hollow bones, and similar ankle joints. These scientists hatched a new idea—birds might be related to dinosaurs!

This idea ruffled feathers in the scientific community. Back then people thought of dinosaurs as giant four-legged beasts that moved slowly and ate plants. Birds were small and fast. Many ate meat. They had feathers, wings, and a wishbone. Dinos did not. So the idea was left to incubate for more than a hundred years.

In 1964, a paleontologist named John Ostrom dug up the fossil of a ***Deinonychus*** in the badlands of Montana, U.S.A. This dinosaur was different. Like ***Archaeopteryx*** and ***Compsognathus***, it was small and stood on two legs. Its skeleton was made for running and jumping, and it had claws for hunting just like birds.

Ostrom wondered if paleontologists like himself had been too chicken to admit those scientists from the 1800s might have been right. Was he foolish to think that some dinosaurs also had feathers, wings, and wishbones like birds? He and others began digging for more clues.

To their surprise, they discovered that some dinosaur fossils already had

wishbones. They had simply been overlooked or mislabeled. Then, in 1996, a farmer in the Liaoning Province of China unearthed the fossil of a ***Sinosauropteryx***, a tiny dinosaur covered in feathery fuzz. Nearby, paleontologists found the fossil of a ***Caudipteryx***, which had feathers identical to present-day birds. Neither of these dinosaurs had wings, though. The years flew by. In 2011, excavators dug up the fossil of a ***Xiaotingia***, a dinosaur with feathered wings capable of flight.

The fossil record finally showed that dinosaurs could be small and fast with feathered wings and a wishbone. Most scientists now agreed that birds, including chickens, were really another kind of dinosaur.

Birds and other dinosaurs lived on Earth until something went wrong, and most living things died suddenly. We don't really know what happened. We do know an enormous rock from outer space smashed into the planet around the same time. That might have done the trick. The only dinosaurs that survived were a small group of birds. They are the ancestors of the over 10,000 species of birds we have today.

Have dinosaurs gone extinct? Absolutely not. No less than 50 billion dinosaurs are roaming Earth today—more than during prehistoric times. In fact, one might be in your backyard right now!

Dinosaur Pronunciations

Archaeopteryx
(ARK-ee-OP-tare-icks)

Argentinosaurus
(ahr-gen-TEEN-oh-SORE-us)

Caudipteryx
(caw-DIP-ter-icks)

Compsognathus
(KOMP-sog-NAH-thus or komp-SOG-no-thus)

Deinonychus
(die-NON-e-kuss)

Dilophosaurus
(DIE-low-fo-SORE-us)

Diplodocus
(dih-PLOD-uh-kus)

Sinosauropteryx
(SINE-oh-sore-OP-ter-iks)

Tyrannosaurus rex
(tye-RAN-oh-SORE-us rex)

Utahraptor
(YOO-tah-RAP-tore)

Velociraptor
(veh-LOSS-ih-RAP-tore)

Xiaotingia
(chow-TING-ee-ah)

Random House Children's Books
A division of Penguin Random House LLC
1745 Broadway, New York, NY 10019
penguinrandomhouse.com
rhcbooks.com

Designed by Brett Challos and
Eva Absher-Schantz

Book team: Katharine Moore, executive editor; Colin Wheeler, photo editor; Lori Epstein, senior photo director; Katherine Kling, fact-checker; Molly Reid, senior copy editor

Library of Congress Control Number: 2025940855
ISBN 978-1-4263-7622-1 (hardcover)
ISBN 978-1-4263-7623-8 (lib. bdg.)

Manufactured in China
10 9 8 7 6 5 4 3 2 1

The authorized representative in the EU for product safety and compliance is Penguin Random House Ireland, Morrison Chambers, 32 Nassau Street, Dublin D02 YH68, Ireland, https://eu-contact.penguin.ie.

Random House Children's Books supports the First Amendment and celebrates the right to read.

Cover (egg), stefanholm/Adobe Stock; (polka-dot pattern), Kuzmick/Adobe Stock; (feet), photomaster/Shutterstock; (background scales), cla78/Shutterstock; (title texture), Anastasiia/Adobe Stock; Back cover, Franco Tempesta/National Geographic Partners, LLC; 1, Kuzmick/Adobe Stock; 1 (BKGRD), cla78/Shutterstock; 2–3 (BKGRD), Oleksandra/Adobe Stock; 3, Mathias Weil/Adobe Stock; 4, Franco Tempesta/National Geographic Partners, LLC; 4–5, (BKGRD), cla78/Shutterstock; 5, Anneka/Shutterstock; 5 (INSET), Frank Rumpenhorst/DPA Picture Alliance/Avalon; 6, Lumos sp/Adobe Stock; 6–7 (BKGRD), BriannaPaige/Adobe Stock; 7, Franco Tempesta/National Geographic Partners, LLC; 8, Franco Tempesta/National Geographic Partners, LLC; 8–9, (BKGRD), Elena/Adobe Stock; 10–11, Tim Plowden/Alamy Stock Photo; 10–11, (BKGRD), Oleksandra/Adobe Stock; 11, Franco Tempesta/National Geographic Partners, LLC; 12–13, Marilyn Barbone/Adobe Stock; 12–13 (BKGRD), Intan Cheria/Adobe Stock; 13, Franco Tempesta/National Geographic Partners, LLC; 14, Franco Tempesta/National Geographic Partners, LLC; 14–15 (BKGRD), BriannaPaige/Adobe Stock; 15, bios48/Adobe Stock; 16–17 (BKGRD), Elena/Adobe Stock; 17, imago stock&people/Avalon; 17 (INSET), Franco Tempesta/National Geographic Partners, LLC; 18–19 (BKGRD), cla78/Shutterstock; 19, Eric Isselee/Shutterstock; 20–21 (BKGRD), Intan Cheria/Adobe Stock; 22–23, Frank Rumpenhorst/DPA Picture Alliance/Avalon; 22–23 (BKGRD), cla78/Shutterstock; 24–25, Jane Burton/Nature Picture Library; 24–25 (BKGRD), Elena/Adobe Stock; 26–27 (BKGRD), cla78/Shutterstock; 27, chamnan phanthong/Adobe Stock; 28–29 (BKGRD), BriannaPaige/Adobe Stock; 29, RubberBall/Alamy Stock Photo; 29 (INSET), purich/Adobe Stock; 30 (LE), IMAGO/Zoonar/christianxdécoutx/Avalon; 30 (RT), Franco Tempesta/National Geographic Partners, LLC; 30–31 (BKGRD), cla78/Shutterstock; 31, Franco Tempesta/National Geographic Partners, LLC; 32, Vladimir Prusakov/Adobe Stock; 32 (BKGRD), cla78/Shutterstock